THE SHAPE OF THINGS

Written by Dave Tovey   Photographs by Douglas Johnson, Cornelia Hasenfuss, and Kevin Larson

Some shapes are circles.

Some are squares.

Some are triangles . . .

that make stairs.

Here are rectangles.

Here are stars.

Here are ovals with some bars.

A semicircle, . . .

. . . diamonds too, . . .

and an octagon . . .

. . . for stopping you.